THE NORM	OUTPERFORM
HOPEFULLY	DEFINITELY
WHEN I HAVE TIME	I'LL MAKE IT A PRIORITY
EXCUSES	ACCOUNTABILITY
I HAVE TO	I GET TO
COMFORTABLE	CHALLENGED
SECURE DECISIONS	CALCULATED RISKS
SOMEDAY	TODAY
GIVEN	EARNED
EASY WAY	BEST WAY
RESOURCES	RESOURCEFULNESS
PLAY NOT TO LOSE	PLAY TO WIN
FOCUSED ON ME	FOCUSED ON WE
FOLLOWER	LEADER

ISBN-13: 978-1981525522
ISBN-10: 1981525521
1st edition, December 2017

Ellie,

You're an Outperformer!

SW

To the student athlete who is reading this right now, thank you for giving me the opportunity to help you Outperform.

For bulk pricing on books for your team or school, or to have Scott speak to your athletes, please visit:

OutperformTheNorm.com/books

TABLE OF CONTENTS

OUTPERFORMING BONUSES

*12 Individual Performance Plans in the Champions Playbook

*Peak Performance Assessment

*A hidden secret the pros use to stay motivated (it's controversial)

*Special "Why They Won" Webinar

*MORE video + audio training!

For instant access please visit:

OutperformTheNorm.com/books

Yes, the bonuses are free. Go get them now.

INTRODUCTION

It was the third quarter of the 1998 Minnesota AAA State Championship football game. We (Albany Huskies) were playing in the Metrodome, the stadium where the Minnesota Vikings played. We had been the #1 ranked team in our class all year. I was a senior cornerback and was mostly responsible for stopping the opposing team from passing on us. We had a comfortable lead in the game, and I found myself letting my mind wander to the postgame party and how sweet it was going to be to celebrate with my teammates, friends, and family.

Before I knew it, our opponent, Jackson County Central, scored a touchdown. They called two play-action passes, and I'd gotten burned both times because I'd mistakenly come up to stop the run. I didn't do my job. I'd gotten out of my zone and lost focus.

Fast forward to the winter season. I was captain of the basketball team and we were fresh off our first state tournament appearance the previous year. As you'll learn later in this book, being a captain meant I was an "Appointed Leader," but I really wasn't ready to lead. I had no idea how to help others raise their game and elevate their play. I took practice and games too seriously and was overly critical when teammates would make mistakes because I *thought* this would make them better. I was wrong. There wasn't a lot of team unity, and consequently, we underperformed and were upset by an inferior opponent early in the playoffs.

Spring was home to my favorite sport, golf. To my knowledge, I'm the only golfer in Albany history to qualify for five straight state golf tournaments. I was coming off of a third place finish as a junior, and I was the favorite to win the state championship that year. But instead of being energized by the opportunity to excel, I felt the heat. It seemed like a suffocating pressure to perform in *every tournament* I played in. I was mentally burned out all year and more nervous than usual because I was solely fixated on outcomes, and whether I won or lost a tournament. In the state championship, I played two of my worst rounds of the season and faded to a 10th-place finish.

Why am I sharing these stories with you? It's simple: I don't want you to repeat my mistakes.

Now, to my credit, I DID do some things well. I worked hard and tried my best in every sport I played. In the same way, I'm sure you work hard and are doing plenty of things well also. You wouldn't have this book in your hands if you weren't already an Outperformer.

But what could you be doing even BETTER?

Sometimes I find myself clinging to the classic line, *"If I knew then, what I know now, everything would have been different."*

That's not entirely true. I have no way of knowing if *everything* would have been different. I can't control outcomes. My win-loss record and individual statistics may have been exactly the same.

What I can guarantee is that, had I known how to focus, be a better leader, embrace nerves, and play to win instead of playing not to lose (just to name a few), I would have given myself **the best possible chance to have success**. Whether this translates into state championships, college scholarships, playing professionally, or making the team is irrelevant.

Those are outcomes and I can't control them. Neither can you.

It is an important distinction: this book is for performance enhancement. It is about maximizing your abilities and individual potential – not about curing an underlying deficiency. Many people shy away from sport psychology programs because there is a stigma that you must be "broken" or there must be something "wrong" with you if you're practicing mental training.

Question: *What percentage of success in your sport do you think is mental (as opposed to physical)?*

I've asked this question to, literally, thousands of athletes over the years and, regardless of their sport, their answer is never less than 50%.

Then consider: *If 50%, or greater, of success in your sport is mental, how much TIME do you devote to mental training?*

The answer is usually not enough...or sometimes none at all.

Being unbeatable from the neck down cannot happen without first being unbeatable from the neck up. If the best athletes on the planet are ALL training their mind to enhance their performance in training and competition, doesn't it make sense that you should do the same?

This book is about knowing you've left it all out there on the field, ice, pool, court, course, or classroom.

It's about being YOUR very best in everything you do.

I'm glad you're here. Let's get after it.

Scott

THE OUTPERFORMER'S CREED

Outperforming isn't a destination.
IT'S A WAY OF LIFE.

You'll never **FEEL READY** for something you **HAVEN'T DONE**

BE A **PILLAR** OF **POSITIVITY**

You have *enough time* for your priorities.
WHAT ARE THEY?

LIGHTEN UP, LAUGH AT YOUR IMPERFECTIONS

Why Not **YOU?** CHANGE ≠ **WORSE**

WE > ME   EMBRACE   THE SUCK   YOU'RE **WORTH IT**

GIVE AND YOU SHALL RECEIVE

Look up from your phone **and greet a stranger.** THEY'RE SOMEBODY.

PAY THE PRICE OF
ADMISSION

OVERNIGHT SUCCESS TAKES *years* OF HARD WORK.

SMILE. ◼
◼ **SWEAT.**
SERVE. ◼

FUEL YOUR BODY, NOURISH YOUR BRAIN

HIGH achievement & fulfillment **ARE MEANT TO GO hand-in-hand**

Make the most of your precious days on this planet
Never put **OTHERS DOWN** to pull you up

Let your **WEIRDO LIGHT** shine bright

LEAVE A LEGACY

Strive for **PROGRESS,** *not perfection*

PLAY **TO WIN**

TAKE NOTHING FOR GRANTED

BE WHO YOU SAY **YOU ARE**

BRING THE JOY   **LAY ONE BRICK EVERYDAY**

LEADERS ARE **READERS.** **LEARNERS** ARE **EARNERS.**

THERE IS NO FAILURE *only feedback*
IT WON'T BE EASY BUT IT WILL BE **WORTH IT**

Have **FUN.** Take **RISKS.** Love **PEOPLE.**

BE DRIVEN BY **DESIRE,** NOT PARALYZED **BY FEAR**

START!

NO GOAL IS TOO LOFTY IF YOU HAVE AN INTELLIGENT PLAN *to accomplish it*
LISTEN AND ACCEPT OTHERS, even when their opinions differ from yours

THE GREATEST PRESENT IS YOUR PRESENCE

Self-limiting beliefs ARE THE GOVERNOR ON YOUR POTENTIAL

Don't wait until someday. **DO IT NOW!**

SUCCESS IS A TEAM SPORT

CHOOSE AN ATTITUDE OF **GRATITUDE**

STEP IT ÛP. Today is game day.

1

COMMIT. COMPETE. SUCCEED.

An Outperformer commits with head,
competes with heart and succeeds with humility.

What do Outperformers do differently than average athletes? How do they commit? Compete? Succeed? What is the MINDSET of a champion?

First, you condition the mind like you condition the body. Think of it this way: You can't hit the weight room once and expect that you're going to be strong. You also can't run once and expect that you're going to be fit and fast. Success is something that happens progressively over time. It's the end result of discipline, dedication, and commitment.

That same process applies to conditioning the mind for peak performance. It requires and ongoing, consistent effort forged over time.

The initial step is COMMIT. We've learned more about the human brain in the last 10-15 years than we've learned in the last

500 years, and the first part of achieving anything is to COMMIT to it. That may sound painfully simple to you, but without it, nothing else matters beyond this point. Goals, motivation, confidence, grit and resiliency are each useless without the decision to commit.

Many people confuse being interested with being committed. When you're interested, you hope and wish that good things happen. You'll take action when it's convenient. You'll go above and beyond when you feel like it. You'll do things when they're easy.

When you're committed, you MAKE good things happen. You get it done, even when it's inconvenient. You give your best, even when you don't feel like it. You do things when they're hard.

This is about your own internal dialogue. For example, you'll say to yourself:

*"I'm **committed** to being positive every single day."*

*"I'm **committed** to staying focused for the entire season."*

*"I'm **committed** to getting stronger in the weight room."*

In the last sentence, when you're committed, you'll go to the weight room even when your schedule is busy. You'll go alone. You'll go when no one else is holding you accountable. You'll go when it seems like you're wasting your time and not getting stronger. You'll go when you're tired and unmotivated. You'll go when you'd rather be doing something else.

You'll go because you're COMMITTED.

Different regions of the brain fire when you use more empowering word choices. [1] Phrases such as *"I'm committed,"* instead of *"I hope," "I would like to,"* or *"I want to,"* actually positively alter your brain and body on a cellular level. The key is to start each sentence with, *"I'm committed to..."*

*"**I'm committed to** having fun."*

*"**I'm committed to** making the team."*

*"**I'm committed to** working hard."*

*"**I'm committed to** being all-conference."*

*"**I'm committed to** being a positive person."*

*"**I'm committed to** winning a state title."*

Constantly saying to yourself, *"I'm committed to,"* is going to strengthen your level of resolve and determination to get to your goal. THAT is everything in life. Without the initial commitment, what follows is irrelevant.

The second step is COMPETE. When I was playing sports at a high level growing up I remember my Mom telling me before big games or competitions:

"Just try your best out there!"

At the time that philosophy didn't make sense to me. I thought "trying my best" didn't matter if that didn't translate to winning.

To compete fully is to give your best at all times. No one else can ever tell you if you've genuinely tried your best, or hardest, at something other than YOU. Your teammates, other students, parents and coaches can't tell you that. Only you know whether you've given your 100% focus, energy, and effort.

Of all the athletes with whom I've worked – whether it's student athletes trying to make a team or professional-level athletes –

they all say that you will be able to accept any result as long as you can look in the mirror afterwards and say to yourself:

"I tried my best out there. I gave it 100% of my effort and skill."

The beautiful thing about competing in this way is, more often than not, it produces the outcomes you want. But life doesn't always follow a perfect Hollywood script, and inevitably, you will have days where you compete with every single fiber of your being and empty every ounce of energy you have in your tank, and still lose. Having the satisfaction of knowing you tried your best lessens the sting and allows you to be comfortable with any result. It doesn't mean you *like it*; but you do *accept it*. You did everything you could and left it all out there.

The final step is SUCCEED. Here's the truth: If you follow the strategies I'm going to share with you in the next 11 chapters, you WILL achieve higher levels of performance. I guarantee it. You'll be a mentally stronger athlete and you'll improve faster.

I'm a big believer that there is no maintaining. We're always either progressing or regressing in athletics, academics and life. A huge part of success is continuing to set more difficult and lofty goals and strive for higher levels of achievement. Especially in sports, where you're competing against other athletes, when you stop progressing others begin achieving more, and you are left regressing. It's important to challenge yourself and avoid complacency.

Long-term success requires you to answer the following question every day:

*"How can I be better **today** than I was **yesterday**?"*

It's only one simple, open-ended question, but it's the daily dose of self-reflection that all Outperformers use to succeed.

GAME RAISING REMINDERS

✓ Don't be interested. Be COMMITTED. It is an initial decision that must be made.

✓ When you COMPETE, give all of your energy, focus, and effort. When you do this, you'll be able to handle any result.

✓ To SUCCEED, there is no maintaining. Stay hungry and continue to challenge yourself with loftier goals and ambitions.

PERFORMANCE PLAN

❶ Name 3 things that you're committed to and *be specific*! What will you do? Who will you be? How will you act?

❷ What is ONE thing you can do today to be better than you were yesterday?

Download all Performance Plans in the Champion's Playbook at:
OutperformTheNorm.com/books

WHY THEY WON

It's difficult to find an athlete that has committed, competed and succeeded better than the New England Patriots' quarterback Tom Brady. He will never go down as one of the greatest athletes ever (look up his 40-yard dash video on YouTube from the NFL combine if you want a chuckle!) but he will go down as one of the greatest *winners* ever. After being selected in the sixth round of the NFL draft, having been passed over by all the teams multiple times, he has gone on to win four Super Bowls, 14 division titles, 12 pro bowl appearances and more playoff wins than any quarterback in NFL history.[2]

The secret of his success comes from his commitment. His recent book, The TB12 Method, details the lengths he goes to in making sure his body and his mind are at peak performance. This includes a crazy strict diet, hydration, a rigid daily routine, performance sleepwear and non-traditional "muscle pliability" workouts, all geared towards helping him play his position better, for longer, than anyone ever has before him.

Do you need to go to these extreme lengths to enhance your own performance? Probably not. But it speaks to the *daily* decisions and commitments that great athletes make each day. Tom also competes with a ferocious desire each time he steps onto the field and, despite his huge success, he succeeds because he never stops trying to improve and master his craft. It's something from which we can ALL learn.

2

OWNING AND SMASHING YOUR GOALS

An Outperformer knows what they want
and creates a precise plan to make it happen.

Think about the last time you were in a car and you needed to get somewhere, but you didn't know how to get there. What's the first thing you did? Probably input the address into your GPS, right? The GPS then gives you the route and the turn-by-turn directions to arrive at your specific destination.

That's how goal setting works. If you don't take the time to set goals, you're getting in your car and aimlessly driving, without knowing where you want to go and how you're going to get there. You're wasting time. You're not efficient and effective.

Goal setting maximizes what you do. All Outperformers have goals in athletics (and in life). It is a critical component to success.

I'm going to walk you through the basic OPP (Outcome, Performance, Process) framework that Outperforming athletes use. It's a simple one to follow, and it will change the way you look at goal setting.

The first part of the OPP framework is Outcome Goals. These are the goals that most athletes set. They are tied to a RESULT. For example:

"I won the game or lost the game."

"I made the team or got cut from the team."

"I finished first or finished worst."

Outcome goals are great because they provide motivation and direction, but they are problematic because **you only have indirect control over whether you actually achieve them.**[3]

Let's say I'm a high-level runner and I want to win the state championship in the one-mile. I can set a PR and run the fastest race of my life but if the other competitors happen to also run their personal bests (and are faster on that day), then I'm resting my entire goal setting success on an outcome that I can't control.

I can hear you saying:

"But, Scott, I can control that outcome! I would just need to run faster than everyone else!"

Sorry, but you're wrong. Can you CONTROL what other people are doing? Unless you have some voodoo-tele-kinetic power that I'm not aware of, you cannot. You have no influence over other people.

Outcome Goals are great. You DO need them. They're a good place to start, but they require something underneath them, and that is where Performance Goals become necessary.

Performance Goals are tied to your own previous standards of performance. Performance Goals fuel Outcome Goals.

Let's say that you're a basketball player and you want to make the All-Conference team. Achieving All-Conference is an Outcome Goal. You can't control what other players in the conference are doing. But you can assess the other players in the conference and say:

"I know if I want to make All-Conference, I'm probably going to need to average 20 points per game."

If last year you averaged 18 points per game, how are you going to level that up? Performance Goals would be:

"I want to improve my points per game from 18 to 20."

"I want to improve my free throw percentage from 60% to 70%."

"I want to improve my 3-pt percentage from 40% to 45%."

Performance Goals are based on self-improvement and what YOU have done in the past. It's you against you. These goals are more controllable and easier to wrap your hands around. You're more focused on what you're doing and not worried about everyone else.

The last piece of goal setting is Process Goals. This is what you DO on a day-to-day basis. It is your daily training, practicing, opening up the weight room, drills, skill work, etc. It's all of the different things that, if you commit to them and do them *really well*, will end up making your Performance Goals inevitable (and, likely, your Outcome Goals too).

In the previous example, you're not going to wake up and magically go from being a 60% free throw shooter to a 70% free throw shooter. You will need Process Goals to make it happen, such as:

"I will practice 20-minutes-a-day on free throws."

"I will work with a shooting coach for one hour each week."

"I will do slow-motion video analysis of my form each month to tweak and improve my technique."

You have 100% control over each of these things. They are actions, and no one can stop you from doing any of them.

Trust me, of all the high-level athletes I've ever worked with or studied, an unwavering commitment to the Process Goals and doing the actions on a daily, weekly, and monthly basis ends up making your Performance Goals and Outcome Goals inevitable. It's a simple, highly effective framework that is beautiful in its simplicity.

Two more important goal setting notes:

First, make sure that your goals are YOUR goals. In other words, your goal setting should not be based on what someone else *thinks* you should do. Anytime you're setting goals, you should always ask yourself whether it's something that you genuinely want? Don't let other athletes, students, parents or coaches put pressure on you and tell you what you should want to achieve. This is your life!

Second – and this is contrary to what most people advise – I encourage you to be somewhat UNREALISTIC in your goals (yes, you heard that correctly!). If you look at anybody that's ever accomplished *anything* significant in life, or in athletics, and chances are it was viewed as unrealistic at some point in time.

I'm a firm believer that ANY goal is realistic if you construct an intelligent plan to accomplish it.

In the *Why They Won* at the end of last chapter I gave the example of Tom Brady. How realistic is it that a 6th round draft pick in the NFL will go on to become the greatest quarterback ever? It's COMPLETELY unrealistic...and anybody who tells you they saw it coming is not being truthful.

In your case, you may have barely made the team last year, and now you want to be All-Conference this year. Good – GO FOR IT! It might seem unrealistic right now, but if you take the time to determine your Performance Goals and then map out the actionable, controllable Process Goals, who is to say that Outcome Goal is unrealistic?

The OPP Goal Setting framework is powerful. It's your secret weapon in high achievement. It answers the question, *"How can I get from point A to point B?"* and can be used in athletics, academics and life. If used effectively, you'll be in a position to accomplish more than you ever thought possible.

GAME RAISING REMINDERS

✓ Outcome Goals provide motivation and direction, but they are problematic because you only have indirect control over them.

✓ Performance Goals are based on improving your own individual previous standards of performance. They fuel Outcome Goals.

✓ Process Goals are ALWAYS 100% in your control, and they are the daily, weekly, and monthly, activities that will lead to you achieving your Performance Goals.

✓ Make sure your goals are YOUR goals. No one else's.

✓ Any goal is realistic if you construct an intelligent plan to accomplish it.

PERFORMANCE PLAN

❶ What is one Outcome Goal you'd like to achieve this year?

❷ What are the Performance Goals that will fuel this Outcome Goal (list 2-3)? In other words, what are your previous benchmarks or stats and how much will you need to improve them?

❸ What are your daily, weekly and monthly Process Goals (list at least 3)? What are the actions and activities that will lead to improved Performance Goals?

Download all Performance Plans in the Champion's Playbook at:
OutperformTheNorm.com/books

WHY THEY WON

When Leicester City won the Premier League in 2015, it was the greatest upset in sports history. Not just in soccer (or European football) history...in SPORTS history. Nothing else has even come close.

Consider how "realistic" this is...

At the beginning of the season they were 5,000-to-1 underdogs.[4] As a basis of comparison, take the worst team (or worst player) in your favorite sport – their odds of winning the championship are still at least 10x better than Leicester City's. It's more likely that Kim Kardashian will be elected our next president than Leicester City would win the Premier League!

What made their championship so remarkable was the fact that it wasn't a one-time victory. It wasn't the "Miracle on Ice," where the U.S. defeated the Soviet Union in hockey in a single game. It was a 9-month season that required repeated victories and Outperforming.

How did they do it? By constructing an intelligent plan to accomplish their goal (NO GOAL is out of reach when you have this, right?). They gave up possession and passing accuracy for a more counter-attack, direct style of play, thus maximizing the players' strengths on the team. They made very few lineup changes throughout the course of the season so the team had a chance to gel and gain familiarity with each other. And they made it fun and rewarding, often giving the players free pizza when they kept "clean sheets."

These performance and process goals were in their control, and most importantly, the goals were theirs. If Leicester City had listened to everyone else and not owned their own PERSONAL goals, this story would never be written.

3

MASTERING MOTIVATION

An Outperformer fuels their motivational fire from within.

Outperformers have the ability to get motivated and stay motivated. They are masters at *creating* motivation. That being said, after observing top-performing athletes for 15+ years, I've learned that NO ONE is motivated all the time. You're going to have days when you don't feel like practicing, training, doing your homework, or competing. It's a part of life.

So, what do you do when you don't feel motivated?

First, focus on posture. Motivation is largely emotional and emotions are created by motions. How you physically hold your body affects your physiology and nervous system, for better or for worse.[5]

Postural positions are also hard-wired into our biology. Think about the last time you won something, whether it was a sporting event, video game, or classroom competition. What was your reaction? Were you hunched forward with your head down, speaking softly? NO! Chances are, you threw your arms up in the air, lifted your head, opened up and raised your voice. Did anyone teach you to act like this when you win something? NO! It's what we instinctively do when we are motivated and feel good about what we've done. These postures are universal.

The good news is that you can reverse engineer this process. The next time you're in one of those "funks" where you don't necessarily feel like doing something, pay careful attention to your posture. You'll likely find that you're walking slower than you usually walk, your head is down slightly, your shoulders are rounded a bit forward, and you're speaking more softly than you normally would. But now that you know the instinctive biological posture we all have when we've Outperformed, all you need to do is mimic that posture and it will produce similar motivational emotions. This means having your head up, chest out, shoulder blades back, and walking and talking a bit faster. You'll notice that this gives you more authority and confidence, and it changes the emotions inside of your body.

Second, we're creatures of habit. We are what we repeatedly do, consistently, over time. It's never been easier to find media (music, videos, articles, podcasts) in the motivational space, literally, on command. If you don't have one already, pick a favorite quote, print it out and have that quote *somewhere* where you can see it. It can even be the wallpaper on your phone, but have it somewhere where it serves as a constant motivational reminder for you.

My favorite quote is by former Alabama football coach, Paul "Bear" Bryant:

"Winning is not normal and people who constantly win do so by following an abnormal path. The discipline and dedication and sacrifices are incomprehensible to the thousands, standing outside looking in, who are capable of joining, yet unwilling to pay the price of admission."

When I hear or see that quote, it strikes a chord in me and gets me motivated. It fires me up! It's almost like the quote is speaking directly to me. Your quote should do the same for you.

In addition to a power quote, other motivational media can be:

- *A scene from a movie*
- *A song*
- *A video on YouTube*
- *A podcast*
- *A passage from a book*

Whatever you choose, have it ready, on demand. In those times where you're not feeling your best, you'll need to come back to it again and again. Even the highest-performing athletes and business leaders on the planet need these things to pick them up.

I've coached a lot of runners and triathletes in recent years. I often tell them that anybody can swim, bike and run when they fresh and rested, and the weather is 70 degrees and sunny, with no wind and low humidity. That takes no talent. But what do you do when you're tired, fatigued and sore, then you look outside and it's cold and raining, with 25 mph gusts of wind?

THAT is where you need to use these strategies to create motivation.

In your shoes, anybody can work out and have great practices, competitions and study sessions when they're feeling their best. But the mark of a true Outperformer is someone who can show up, motivated, and do the job when they don't have "it." You learn a lot more about yourself during these times of internal struggle and adversity.

GAME RAISING REMINDERS

✓ Posture affects physiology. Stand tall. Head up, chest out, shoulder blades back, and walk and talk like you're a real deal Outperformer (because you ARE!).

✓ Pick out your favorite motivational quote and have it visible DAILY. Your locker, backpack, phone wallpaper, car, bedroom, wallet, purse, etc., are all great examples.

✓ Strategically use your favorite media (movie scenes, songs, videos, podcasts, book passages, etc.) to pick you up when you're not on your game and feeling your best.

PERFORMANCE PLAN

❶ What will you do to remind yourself of having a power posture (be specific)?

❷ What is your favorite piece of motivational media (quote, song, movie, video, etc.) and how will you strategically use it to enhance your motivation?

Download all Performance Plans in the Champion's Playbook at:
OutperformTheNorm.com/books

WHY THEY WON

Michael Jordan remembered every person who doubted him (including his coach who cut him from the varsity team) and used it as motivation to become the greatest NBA player ever.

When Stephen Ames publicly criticized how Tiger Woods was hitting the golf ball prior to the 2006 Match Play Championship, Tiger used it as motivation to beat Ames 9 & 8, the most lopsided result possible in match play.

Sidney Crosby's motivation comes from the fear that one of the younger players will outwork him and surpass him as the NHL's best player.

Tom Brady still plays with a chip on his shoulder and has never forgotten all the teams that passed him over – multiple times – on his way to being a 6th round NFL draft pick.

Tennis great Roger Federer stays motivated by "Kaizen" (continuous improvement) and the belief that someday he might be able to play a "perfect game." Annika Sorenstam, one of the greatest female golfers of all time, believed the same thing – that there was the possibility for a "perfect round."

Heck – even my high school football team used to watch the movie *"The Program"* every Friday afternoon to motivate us before our games!

The common thread in all of these examples is the strategic, intentional use of motivation. It doesn't just "happen." All of these athletes (and teams) know exactly what revs their motor and they tap into it continuously to perform their best. So should you.

4

PRACTICING WITH A PURPOSE

*An Outperformer is too fixated on improving
to waste time coasting and going through the motions.*

When you look at the athletes who are successful in sports, do they spend more time practicing their sport than average or lesser successful athletes? Yes, absolutely. They arrive earlier and stay later, "punching in" and "punching out" for longer hours than others.

Malcolm Gladwell popularized this notion of "10,000 hours" in his book, *Outliers,* where he studied and found that world-class performers all hit this critical threshold of time allocated to their craft.[6] Because of it, you had scores of athletes believing that if they "go through the motions" for 10,000 hours, they'd achieve mastery and become world-class too.

What was mostly overlooked in *Outliers* is that Outperformers are also much more efficient and effective with the *time* they spend practicing. They are engaged physically AND mentally, and because of this, they maximize their ROI (*Return on Invest-*

ment), which should be the primary objective of any athlete. If you can get a greater return (performance improvement) on your investment (time and energy), you'll achieve higher levels of success faster and easier.

It makes sense – why would you want to spend more time than necessary to improve?

One of the books that opened my eyes to this was Daniel Coyle's book, *The Talent Code*. He looked at the different pockets and cultures that were producing world-class athletes in many different sports. He wanted to know what these people were doing differently in the time that they trained and practiced. One of the biggest observations he made was that struggle is a GOOD thing.[7]

I often tell people that mastery comes on the other side of struggle, and struggling is *required* if you want to improve and refine your skills. Unfortunately, in our society, we often look at making mistakes, or struggling, as failures. We perceive it as negative. But Coyle found that you learn up to 10x faster when you're operating at the edge of your abilities. This means you push yourself to be better when you get comfortable being uncomfortable.

Let's say as a basketball player, you're capable of easily making a left-handed layup. Well, if you continue to do nothing but to shoot that same left-handed layup, you're not going to learn any new skills and you won't improve as rapidly because you're not stretching your current abilities. But if you try a crossover dribble between your legs and then shoot that left-handed layup, you've added a new element to the mix that challenges you. You might get called for traveling, lose the ball out of bounds, turn the ball over to the other team or miss the layup, and all of those are GOOD things.

A phrase to repeat to yourself is:

"There is no failure; there's only feedback."

If you can embrace this concept you will no longer look at mistakes as negative failures. You will look at them as positive growth opportunities. When you do this, you will maximize the efficiency and the effectiveness of your practice and training time because you'll be operating at the edge of your abilities. You'll be doing the right things and doing the things right. You'll be gathering essential feedback that is leading you one step closer to mastery.

The second parts of *Practicing with a Purpose* are to "chunk it out" and "slow it down." You do not necessarily want to look at a technique, or skill, as a *complete movement*. For example, if you're trying to improve your running stride, you don't want to operate in generalities, such as *"I'm just trying to run better."* WHAT does that mean? HOW are you trying to run better?

You also don't want to focus on too many things at once. World-class technique comes from a series of separate, yet integrated, components performed with precision. You cannot think about your arm swing, foot strike, push off, breathing, knee lift, posture, etc., *simultaneously.* If you're thinking of all these different things, you'll get paralysis by analysis and you'll end up doing NOTHING well.

So, if you want to improve as a runner, chunk out the movements. You might start by focusing on being more relaxed in your hands for a better arm swing. When you're doing this, you not worried about your legs, breathing or posture, even if you know in the back of your mind that you're not doing them particularly well. **Give this ONE movement your 100% focus and undivided attention!** Then, after you've spent time working on it, move onto your foot strike (the next "chunk") and do the same thing. Continue working through the process until you've covered ALL the essential components of your technique.

This is what all Outperforming athletes do and, as a side note, it's a fantastic example of what could go into your process goals. It's an anti-"going through the motions" approach that allows you to improve faster.

Next, one of the worst mistakes you can make is to attempt to perform a movement at full speed if you're trying to make a technique change or ingrain a new skill. It is better to slow it down to whatever speed you need to (it can be half-speed or quarter-speed) so you can **perform the new motion absolutely perfectly.**

Most people overlook this key concept when they're trying to refine their technique. Back in the days when Tiger Woods was dominating golf, I read stories about him spending hours in front of a mirror *swinging at half-speed* trying to ingrain a new movement in his swing.[8] Once you become more comfortable and the technique change starts to feel second nature, then you can gradually ramp up the speed to "game speed." But don't rush this process! You're much better off starting too slowly and doing it perfectly then you are rushing it too fast and being sloppy.

Practice doesn't make perfect; Perfect practice makes perfect.

The last strategy is to watch great athletes *intently.* When I say "watch," I don't mean just sitting there and casually observing them doing their thing, whether that is running, swinging a golf club, kicking a field goal, hitting a slap shot, pitching a baseball, nailing a backhand, shooting a free throw, or anything else. That's what 'The Norm' does. Outperformers *study* other great athletes with such focus and concentration that they're almost in a hypnotized state. They're honed in on the specific, precise movements and details of what the athlete is doing. They, then, take this information and mimic it in their own technique.

Later, you'll learn that making things happen in reality first starts by making them happen in your mind, and watching great athletes and how they do, what they do, is vital to *Practicing with a Purpose*. It strengthens the neural pathways in your brain that allow you to take that information back and use it in your own personal performance. You'll improve faster, and easier, with less time and energy expended.

GAME RAISING REMINDERS

✓ Outperformers get more return (performance improvements) from their investment (time and energy). That's a big reason why they achieve world-class levels.

✓ There is no failure; there is only feedback. Struggle is required. It is a GOOD thing.

✓ Chunk it out. Take ONE specific component of your technique that you're trying to improve and isolate it. Give it your 100% singular focus and effort. Then, rinse and repeat for the other components.

✓ Slow it down to the point that you can execute any form or technique change absolutely perfectly. It doesn't matter how slow you go starting out. You can layer on the speed later.

PERFORMANCE PLAN

❶ What is one area of your technique you'd like to improve? Be *very specific* on this area. What drill or part of practice can you use to most effectively work on this?

❷ Who is an athlete that you can study intently to learn from their technique?

Download all Performance Plans in the Champion's Playbook at:
OutperformTheNorm.com/books

WHY THEY WON

Michael Phelps is considered, almost inarguably, the greatest swimmer of all time with 28 Olympic medals. People want to laud his wingspan, ankle flexibility and height (all beneficial traits for swimming at a high level) but no one saw what happened behind closed doors.

Phelps' practice habits have become legendary. According to his coach, Bob Bowman, Michael didn't miss a practice for FOUR YEARS leading up to the 2004 Olympics.[9] Yes, that's 365 days a year. Even on holidays, he trained. He never missed a single day.

Beyond the *quantity* of his practice, Phelps was obsessive about the *quality* of his practice. Bowman has also called him "the most goal-oriented person on the planet." He had clearly defined goals for each practice – what area of his technique he was going to focus on and exact split times for each set and stroke. Because of this, he minimized "going through the motions" and maximized his efficiency for each practice. It was his path to continued improvement.

5

UNLEASHING THE ALPHA DOG

An Outperformer overrides fear with ironclad faith
and an unwavering belief—in themselves.

Not long ago, I was helping a triathlete get ready for an Ironman (140.6 miles of swimming, biking and running). She
was coming back from a stress-fracture injury in her femur, but
she was used to winning or placing on the podium in her age
group. As she was getting ready for the race, she started to doubt
her own abilities, specifically on the bike and run. Even though
she'd trained solidly for the previous 3+ months, she didn't have
confidence that she could *still* beat the athletes that she normally
beats in races.

I sent her a text message on the morning of the race that said:

"You're the alpha dog. Remember that. You've competed against all the-
se people before. They have to come up to your level. Trust your prepara-
tion and go out there and do what you do and race like you've always
done. Do that and the rest will take care of itself."

Sure enough, she went out and smashed her expected finishing time. She didn't finish on the podium but she set a personal best and had a fantastic race.

Unleashing the Alpha Dog is generating the confidence necessary to be successful in sports and life. You show me any successful person and I will show you someone who has tremendous self-confidence. It's a non-negotiable trait that you must have to Outperform.

Just so we're on the same page, confidence is NOT the same as arrogance. The difference? Arrogant people think they know it all. They're cocky. They believe there's nothing more to learn. They feel they're above others. They brag. Especially in my home state of Minnesota, many people are so afraid of coming across as arrogant that they intentionally hide and downplay their own self-confidence (what we refer to as "Minnesota polite").

Confidence is simply a faith and belief in your own abilities. It's arrogance under control.

There are four ways to enhance your level of confidence when you start to doubt yourself. The first one is to adopt a Power Posture. This was covered extensively in *Mastering Motivation*, and it also applies to confidence. In any moment, if you want to feel more confident, stand up taller, with head up, chest out, shoulder blades back, and start walking and talking like you mean it. Never forget the power of your posture! Trying to be an alpha dog with a scared kitten posture is trying to jam a square peg in a round hole. It just doesn't fit.

Secondly, confidence is built by trusting in your preparation and practicing like you're going to perform. They are dress rehearsals for game day. For example, a basketball player who is worried about being able to shoot free throws when he's tired at the end of the game will need to specifically prepare for that moment. Practice running yourself to a point where you're tired and then immediately shoot free throws *with some type of added consequence if you miss* (more running, pushups, etc.). You need to KNOW what it feels like to be in that situation. When you do this, it enhances your self-confidence and becomes a reservoir that you can go back to and draw from in your preparation.

This is the exact reason that NFL football teams will pipe in crowd noise and blaring music for practice when their next game is being played in a loud stadium. They know that it's going to be difficult to hear the signals and calls, and the more that the situational demands mimic what they're going to face in the game and competition, the more confident they're going to be when it matters. The same mentality applies to your own preparation.

Next, enhance your confidence by using Vicarious Experiences. These are based on someone else who has done whatever you are looking to do. Find a person who has performed really well in a game-day situation, or who has taken his or her "game" to another level, that is similar to you. You can draw from their experiences and say:

"If they can do it, I can do it too."

When you do this, it's not putting anyone else down; it's pulling yourself up.

When I ran my 100-mile ultra-marathon, I was scared to death and wondering what the heck I'd gotten myself into. I wasn't confident that I was going to be able to finish it (100 miles is a long ways to run!). Then I remembered vicarious experiences. I looked around at some of the other athletes at the start line, and I said:

"There is absolutely no way that every other person at this race is fitter and more mentally tough than I am. If THEY can run 100 miles, I can run 100 miles too!"

Again, I wasn't putting them down; I was pulling myself up. And I gained confidence from it.

Whatever you're looking to do in athletics or academics, I'm betting someone else has done it before. They're probably no bigger, faster, stronger, smarter, or more talented than you are. Let that pull you up!

Finally, improve your confidence through imagery. This was mentioned briefly in the last chapter on *Practicing with a Purpose*, but there isn't a single Olympic or professional athlete on the planet that doesn't practice imagery. It's a key differentiator between Outperforming and less successful athletes.

The strategy with imagery is to incorporate as many of the senses as possible into your imagery experience:

*What are you going to **see**?*
*What are you going to **smell**?*
*What are you going to **feel**?*
*What are you going to **hear**?*
*What are you going to **experience**?*

Imagery is the perfect thing to do when you're lying in bed the night before you have a big competition or a big game. Try to make your imagery as vivid as possible and literally put yourself

THERE. Mentally rehearse all the different circumstances that you'll face during the game or competition. The clearer you can make it in your mind, the more confidence it will build, and the more it will manifest itself in reality.

GAME RAISING REMINDERS

✓ Confidence is a good thing. It's arrogance under control.

✓ Focus on your Power Posture. It'll immediately change your confidence at any point in time.

✓ Make your preparation a dress rehearsal for game day and trust it! Mimic the specific demands you'll face and you'll be better.

✓ Vicarious Experiences: If someone else can do it, so can you!

✓ Use imagery. Create the competition vividly in your mind, incorporating as many of the senses as possible. See it, feel it, hear it, smell it, experience it.

PERFORMANCE PLAN

❶ What can you do to make your preparation more of a dress rehearsal for game day?

❷ Who else has accomplished what you want? Ideally, don't make this person a pro athlete. Pick someone who is a "level" above you and gain confidence that you can be where they are.

❸ Imagine your next big game or competition – what will you see, smell, hear, feel and experience? Write an imagery script and rehearse it.

Download all Performance Plans in the Champion's Playbook at:
OutperformTheNorm.com/books

WHY THEY WON

At the 2004 Olympic games in Athens, Usain Bolt didn't make it past the first round of the 100m Sprint. Fans booed him, cursed him, and laughed at him.

He didn't care; he knew he would be back. He knew where he was going.

Some would label Usain Bolt as arrogant, but those who know him best say that this isn't how he is at all. He never feels that he's *above* someone else – he is simply ultra-confident in his own abilities and what he is able to do on the track.[10] It has helped make him the greatest sprinter of all time.

There are three lessons we can learn from Usain's confidence:

First, his confidence is built through unwavering commitment and preparation. When he settles into the blocks before a race he knows he's ready. He's been there a thousand times before because he has—literally—practiced a thousand times. His preparation brings familiarity, then confidence, then success.

He's also been there a thousand times in his mind. He pictures the way he wants a race to unfold. He sees himself exploding out of the blocks. He feels his body driving forward to get up to speed and holding his form all the way through the finish line. He hears the runners in the adjacent lanes trying to chase him down. Because he experiences these things in his mind with all his senses, it manifests itself in reality.

Lastly, he doesn't let his detractors bring him down. He's knows who he is and he won't let anyone rain on his parade when they have no parade of their own. He's seen other people, especially Jamaicans, do great things (vicarious experiences) and he chooses to focus on and draw strength from that. Everything else is secondary and unimportant.

6
DEVELOPING GRIT

An Outperformer can't stop—won't stop—until the job is done.

At 3:06am on June 7th, 2015, I crossed the finish line of the Kettle Moraine 100-mile ultra marathon. I had been running for 21 hours and 6 minutes through the hills of southeastern Wisconsin. It was, *by far*, the hardest thing I've ever done in my life.

In the days and weeks that followed, everybody wanted to know my "secret" to running 100 miles. Was I an elite athlete? Did I have a unique training program or a special nutrition plan? They had no idea.

Slumped over, I'm physically and mentally exhausted from running 100 miles

I cannot begin to tell you how many times I wanted to quit during those 100 miles when it was cold, dark and I was exhausted. It would have been so easy to do – more than half of the people that start the race don't finish it. They give up. What got me through was GRIT and the same mental strategies you'll learn in this chapter.

Grit is about rolling up your sleeves, working hard and not stopping until you've accomplished your goal. Unfortunately, in our society, we tend to admire the *after* and fail to acknowledge the *before*. We see a high-level athlete and say:

"Wow! That person came out of nowhere. They're an overnight success!"

What we don't realize is that there are no overnight successes in life. Anybody successful in athletics has been unbelievably gritty. We didn't see where they started. We weren't there for their failures. We can't appreciate how many times they wanted to quit. We have no idea the amount of blood, sweat, and tears that went into this athlete now being at a level where people are calling them an "overnight success."

No one comes from nowhere. We all started somewhere.

There are four ways that you can enhance your level of grit and work ethic. The first is through self-awareness. Our awareness of our own thoughts is one of the greatest skills we can learn. Because of repeated exposure to media, mistakes (perceived as failures and not feedback) and negative people around us, we become conditioned over time to look at the glass as half-empty instead of half-full. It's impossible to be gritty if you're looking at yourself and saying:

"I'm never going to make the team."
"I'm not as talented as this person."
"I'm just wasting my time and not seeing any improvement."

The first step to flipping the grit switch is having an awareness of negative thoughts that aren't serving you. Then, instead of saying these things, you reframe them as:

"I won't stop until I make the team."
"What I lack in talent, I can make up for in hard work."
"If I continue to put in the time, I know it will pay off."

Second, try to avoid social comparison. I understand that this is difficult, especially for young athletes. We're living in an age of social media and always being "compared" to others. But it's not about being better than someone else. It's about being better than YOU were yesterday.

This is where you have to know yourself (again, *self-awareness!*). If looking at other people makes you question your own ability and whether you'll ever reach their level, it's going to demotivate you and detract from your level of grit, thus lowering your individual performance. It IS possible to make positive comparisons, but these comparisons HAVE TO be preceded by empowering thoughts. For example, if you see an athlete who is more talented and skilled than you and say, *"I know that you've got me right now, but I'm coming for you!"* then the comparison is helpful and motivational. You're going to level up and work even harder because you want what that person has...and you believe it can be done.

Third, don't cut corners. This is where grit becomes a muscle. It is something that's strengthened over time by not taking the easy way out. Each time you flex your grit muscle, it gets more developed. This means:

If you have to run an extra sprint at the end of practice, you don't slack off on it. **You do it.**

If you've got an extra set on the bench press or the squat rack, you don't slack off on it. **You do it.**

If you've got an extra 10 problems that need to be completed on your homework assignment, you don't slack off on it. **You do it.**

You build grit each time you do something that you don't want to do and you don't quit when you're 80-90% finished. That last 10-20% means EVERYTHING in life, and you become stronger and better the next time around.

Think about it: Do you *really* want to be known as the person who quits when things get tough? As a person who stops early? As a person who gives up before the finish line?

I doubt it.

Finally, focus on progress, not perfection. No one wants to continually beat their head against a brick wall and feel like they're never getting anywhere. You want to see improvement and break through that wall! You want to know that you're accomplishing something.

To do this, focus on the journey, not on the end destination. Acknowledge and appreciate the progress you're making along the way. Olympic athletes train for *four years* to take *seconds* off of their event time! If they weren't able to focus on the tiniest micro-improvements along the way, there's no way they'd make it to the Games. They'd give up.

Find comfort in the small measures of progress that you're making and recognize that you're better today than you were yesterday (even if only by a fraction). Then, do it again tomorrow. And the next day. If you continue to stack up this work over time and look at life through that lens, I promise your long-term performance will never be the same.

GAME RAISING REMINDERS

✓ Be self-aware of your daily thoughts. Are they serving you and making you better? Or are they hurting you and making you worse?

✓ Avoid social comparison, and if you must do it, make sure it's motivating you. Always strive to be a better version of YOU.

✓ Don't cut corners. The last 10-20% of doing something that you don't want to do flexes and strengthens your grit muscle.

✓ Focus on the journey, not the destination. Each day, lay ONE brick, perfectly. Eventually, you'll have a wall.

PERFORMANCE PLAN

❶ Keep a journal for one day, recording all of your thoughts throughout the course of a day. Then, use it for awareness and reflection. Are these thoughts helping or hurting you?

❷ What is one specific, challenging activity where you PROMISE not to cut corners to strengthen your grit muscle?

Download all Performance Plans in the Champion's Playbook at:
OutperformTheNorm.com/books

WHY THEY WON

Every hockey player in Minnesota knows the story of Jack Jablonski. He was a sophomore at Benilde-St. Margaret's and on course to play Division I hockey in college.

On December 31st, 2011, that all changed.

He was checked from behind into the boards and severed his C5 and C6 vertebrae. He was paralyzed and would never play hockey again. Most doctors think he will never walk again.

A lot has happened in the years since, but instead of mourning his misfortune and lost opportunities, Jack has used his injury as motivation. He's currently a student at USC and has an internship with the L.A. Kings. He's set up his own charity to help people with spinal cord recovery. He conducts his own podcast.

More than anything, he honors the struggle. He continues to engage in rigorous physical therapy three times a week, for two hours each session...even when he's not feeling his best and it would be easy to question whether any of it matters, or is worthwhile.[11] But he finds motivation in helping others and focusing on the progress he's making, not succumbing to social comparison, knowing the athletic "perfection" he once knew will never exist again.

It is a true testament to his grit.

7

BUILDING BULLETPROOF RESILIENCE

*An Outperformer may stumble and fall
but they always rise up.*

You must have the ability to overcome adversity. When you're in the heat of competition and you're struggling, you need to find a way to stay resilient, refocus and bounce back. When you get knocked down, you must get back up.

You've seen it happen plenty of times – a team or an athlete makes a mistake and then they compound it with another, and another, and another...and before you know it they're completely "rattled" and can't get back to playing their game. It's a difficult thing to watch and it's almost completely psychological.

The mind has a funny way of playing tricks on us when things aren't going our way. We become irrational and start creating narratives in our head that aren't truthful. One way to combat this is by Countering, which is the act of making a counter argument against your own negative thinking.

You've probably seen a TV show or movie that features a lawyer arguing the facts in a case. When your mind is telling you, *"I NEVER play well against this team,"* you need to present a factual counter argument against that thought. The counter argument should squash it. You might say something like, *"That's BS. I had one of my BEST games of the season against this team last year!"* Assuming this is truthful, it interrupts your current pattern of thinking and dispels the false story you're telling yourself.

Another way to be more resilient is by using Reference Points. Reference points are times in your life when you've experienced adversity, positively responded to it, and overcame it. You can use this to boost your confidence and as a "reference" to help you move forward in the future.

A few years ago my brother and I were running the Chicago Marathon. I felt good early, but as I got to mile 21, everything started to *just...feel...hard* (I'm sure you've had workouts like that too, right?). The last 5 miles of that race were the most pain and suffering I've ever endured in my life. Thankfully, I had my brother next to me pulling me along but the race forced me to look deep down inside myself to find out how much pain and suffering I could handle and how much adversity I could overcome and still move forward. To this day, I still come back to the Chicago Marathon as a reference point. It doesn't matter if I'm doing another marathon, an Ironman, a 100-mile ultra-marathon, a speech or trying to finish writing a book. I use that memory as a reference point and say, *"I did it before and I can do it again."* That's exactly what you should say to yourself.

The highest performing athletes on the planet all have these reference points. They can recall something in the past that they've had to overcome. They strategically use these reference points as reservoirs of strength and resiliency because they know that if they've done it before, then they can do it again.

If you haven't noticed, your reference point *does not* have to be situation-specific. It can be in ANY area, not just in athletics. But when you get to a point of adversity and you wonder whether you can push through it, you draw strength from the reference point that you CAN. When you do this, what happens is that you respond positively to the challenge and overcome it. In doing so, you establish *another* reference point. It starts a snowball effect and, before you know it, you'll have a wealth of reference points from which to be resilient.

GAME RAISING REMINDERS

✓ If adversity is getting the best of you, use Countering. Be a lawyer and present a factual counter argument to the case going on in your own head.

✓ Establish a Reference Point for a time when you've overcame great adversity in your life. Continually come back to it and say, "If I've done it before. I can do it again."

PERFORMANCE PLAN

❶ Have you ever had a game or a competition where you were struggling and couldn't turn it around? What were your thoughts during this time and how could you have used Countering to enhance your performance?

❷ What's something significant you've had to overcome in your life that you can use as a reference point?

Download all Performance Plans in the Champion's Playbook at:
OutperformTheNorm.com/books

WHY THEY WON

A few years ago, Sloane Stephens was supposed to be the future of American tennis. She upset Serena Williams in the 2013 Australian Open and everyone expected big things.

Shortly thereafter, she started having pain in her left foot. It was a stress fracture. She gave it time to heal and tried to come back to tennis, but unfortunately, the pain came back with it. She had another surgery and was forced to stay completely off of her feet for 12 weeks.

At this point she thought her career might be over.

Can you imagine? You go from being one of the best in the world at your sport to fearing you may *never play again?*

When she started her comeback for the 2017 U.S. Open she was ranked 957th in the world. NO ONE expected her to make any noise. But she displayed a newfound determination and resilience that she never had pre-injury. Instead of being haphazard about her preparation and performance, she now had a new lease on tennis – a second chance – and she was going to make it count.

She stunned everyone by winning the 2017 U.S. Open.

To quote *Sports Illustrated*, "Perhaps the clearest takeaway from the win is how good can result from injury, mistakes, fear and loss; Stephens would never have learned these truths about herself without them: *'That I'm a real fighter, that I have a lot of grit,'* she said. *'Surprising.'"*[12]

8

GETTING IN THE ZONE

An Outperformer is locked in
and laser focused on the task at hand.

Every athlete has heard the phrase "in the zone." You know it when you're there. You also know it when you see it. It's a special state of being cool, calm, and collected, and in complete control of what's going on around you. It feels like time slows down and you're operating at a different speed than other athletes around you. It's one of the most important concepts in all of sport psychology because the more often you can get into the zone, the higher, and more consistent, your performance is going to be.

The problem with getting into the zone is that it's fleeting. There's no sure-fire way to say, *"If you do A, B, and C, you will automatically get in the zone."* It doesn't work that way. Even professional athletes can't get there on command. But there are three things that you should DO, and three things that you should AVOID to give yourself the best chance of getting in the zone and performing your best.

First, have a pre-game or pre-performance routine. This includes EVERYTHING, from what you eat, what you drink, what you wear, what music you listen to and how you warm up. Your entire routine before a game or a competition needs to be dialed in. The reason you do this is because we're all creatures of habit. If you execute a specific peak performance routine where you're always eating, drinking, wearing, listening and doing the same thing, you'll feel a different level of concentration and comfort about what's happening around you.

Second, find the challenge in whatever it is that you're doing. Getting in the zone exists from a balance of challenge and skill level. This is simple if you're competing against another high-level athlete or team. The challenge is readily apparent and obvious. But for athletes and teams who aren't at your "level," it's different. You can't get into the zone if something seems completely easy for you; you're going to end up being bored and apathetic. Some of the greatest athletes of all time (Michael Jordan, Floyd Mayweather, Roger Federer, Tiger Woods) competed regularly against other athletes that weren't at their "level." To facilitate the likelihood of getting in the zone, they had to CREATE some type of challenge to keep them interested. If you want to enhance the probability of the zone occurring, day in and day out, seek the challenge in everything you do.

Third, know your ZOF (Zone of Optimal Functioning). You have to know where you perform your best. Is it more relaxed or more keyed up? Do you like the music blaring before a big competition or do you like being so relaxed that you could take a nap? Once you've identified this, pay attention to your breathing and movements prior to a game and strive to always be at YOUR optimal arousal level. This level is completely individual and unique to you, and it is crucial for being able to get in the zone and perform your best. We'll also discuss this in Chapter 10, *Harnessing Your Nervous Energy*.

As far as the things you must avoid to get in the zone, the biggest mistake I see athletes make is worrying about what other people are doing. Control the controllables! If you're worried about what the competition is doing, you can't possibly be focused on what YOU should be doing. Is there anything you can personally do to control what they're doing? No! You can't control what's going on in the crowd, the calls from the referees, the weather and the conditions of your "playing field." Refocus and control what you can control.

Second thing to avoid is negative self-talk. Instead of telling you "not to think negatively," I recommend having a simple cue of 1-3 words that will immediately help you raise your game. For example:

"Bring it on!"

"Step up!"

"Be present!"

"Game on!"

"You've got this!"

You want to have some type of positive reinforcing message that you're saying to yourself over and over, because any amount of negative self-talk, self-doubt, and lack of self-confidence is going to detract from your ability to get in the zone.

The third thing to avoid is being distracted (or not being present). Growing up as a golfer, I was always given the advice to take it "one shot at a time." This means constantly being in the moment. Whatever has happened, good OR bad, you have to leave it there and be crystal clear on exactly *what is happening right NOW*. Thinking about what has happened in the past and what may happen in the future is useless. Be where you are! You can use the same cue words as you established in the previous point to snap you back into the present moment if you find your focus starting to fade.

GAME RAISING REMINDERS

✓ Have a pre-competition routine and do it the same every time.

✓ Find a challenge in everything you do.

✓ Know your ZOF (Zone of Optimal Functioning) and use breathing and movements to raise or lower your arousal level.

✓ Control the controllables! Worrying about anything other than you is irrelevant.

✓ Avoid negative self-talk. Use a short 1-3 word phrase for positive reinforcement.

✓ Be present and focused on what is happening RIGHT NOW.

PERFORMANCE PLAN

❶ What is your pre-competition routine? What are the actions that you could execute the SAME WAY to help you get in the zone?

❷ On a scale of 1-to-10 (1 being relaxed, 10 being fired up), where do you perform your best? What can you do to make sure you're at your number?

❸ What are your cue words that you can say to yourself to help you stay present and avoid negative self talk?

Download all Performance Plans in the Champion's Playbook at:
OutperformTheNorm.com/books

WHY THEY WON

Steph Curry, guard for the Golden State Warriors and 2-time NBA MVP, has a pre-game routine that is quickly becoming legendary. Fans will show up *more than an hour before tipoff* just to catch a glimpse of it.

Typically, NBA players (especially ones as accomplished as Curry) will start to take their pre-game preparation less seriously. They'll take the court a few minutes before the game starts, hoist a few shots from various positions and do some light stretching to get loosened up. Not Curry. Even though some of the drills he does might seem strange – they are very methodical and purposeful.

Take his pre-game dribbling routine:

- Two balls on either side of his body

- Crossover right to left in front of his body

- Alternate bouncing and through the legs

- Through the legs and behind the back

- Combination of side-to-side, through the legs, behind the back, and front and back[13]

That's it, and it's not so much WHAT he does that matters – it's the WHEN and the HOW. He does it at the same point before every game (and it's the *first* thing he does) and he is disciplined in executing it the same way every time. This repetition enhances his concentration and helps him to feel comfortable; regardless if they're playing home or away, or whether it's a pre-season game or game 7 of the NBA Finals. The comfort of the routine facilitates his ability to get in the zone.

9

HARNESSING YOUR NERVOUS ENERGY

*An Outperformer craves the nervousness from
big competitions—it's exactly where they want to be.*

Think about the last time you were nervous for a game or competition – was it a meaningless scrimmage or something significant? I already know the answer – it is the latter. Whether it's a test, a video game, or a championship game, if you don't care about the outcome, you won't get nervous for it.

Only meaningful things make us nervous. Only big events bring butterflies.

That might sound obvious to you but the first step to harnessing your nervous energy is to pay attention to your *interpretation* of the nervousness. Most people look at nerves as though there's something wrong with them if they're feeling that way. They think it's going to hurt their performance. They automatically associate sweaty palms, a dry mouth and butterflies in their stomach as negatives. IT'S NOT. *Everybody* gets nervous, even elite and professional athletes.

Outperformers, on the other hand, look at nerves as a GOOD thing that's going to help their performance. They flip the switch and say to themselves, *"I can't wait to compete in this BIG game!"* or *"This is GREAT how much nervous energy I have!"* It sounds strange to look at it this way but that's the interpretation and internal dialogue that happens with great athletes.

Next, identify your ZOF (Zone of Optimal Functioning). This was also discussed in the last chapter *Getting In The Zone* and it's the level of arousal, anxiety, and nervous energy you like to feel during games and competitions. Some people like to feel like they're bouncing off the walls; others want to be left alone to stay very calm and relaxed. There isn't a right and a wrong way. It's simply YOUR way and it's critically important to find your ZOF where you perform and function your best.

To go a little deeper, the physiology of nerves happens mostly in the sympathetic nervous system, which is why we are consciously manipulating it to find our ZOF.[14] If you are someone that functions better at the lower end of the arousal scale, focus on taking long, slow, deep breaths. Also make an intentional effort to slow down your pre-competition movements. Walk slower and talk slower. Be more deliberate in your actions. Doing these things will help you feel more relaxed. If you're a higher-strung person you want to do the exact opposite. Be very purposeful and energetic in your movements. Let the energy move you. Fast-paced music is also a great thing to use, as it's typically easier to increase your arousal level with music than it is to decrease it.

Lastly, try to remove the outcomes and focus on the processes. When we get really nervous about ANYTHING, it's almost always because we're fixated on the OUTCOME. We worry:

"What grade am I going to get on the test?"

"Am I going to make the team?"

"Are we going to win or lose this championship game?"

Outcome. Outcome. Outcome. Our nerves are tied to results, which in sports, usually translates to winning and losing. You probably remember from the *Owning and Smashing Your Goals* chapter that we only have indirect control over outcomes in our lives. We need to refocus on controlling the controllables and one thing that you can *always* control is the process. So, before a big competition, the processes are the actions that are going to facilitate the outcome. These are always things over which you have 100% control.

For example, if you're a sprinter, instead of being nervous about winning or losing the race, your process might be to focus on a strong push off out of the blocks, a big powerful arm swing, keeping the heap down early, and staying tall as you near the finish line. All of these different processes are 100% in your control and they remove you from worrying about the outcome.

GAME RAISING REMINDERS

✓ Outperformers INTERPRET their nerves differently. They see nerves as a positive that will help their performance. 'The Norm' sees nerves as a negative that will hurt their performance.

✓ Identify your ZOF and be intentional about raising or lowering your arousal level to where you perform best. Use breathing, movements and music to make this happen.

✓ Remove the outcomes and focus on the process and the actions that are 100% in your control.

PERFORMANCE PLAN

❶ When is the last time you were really nervous for something? What did you say to yourself about the nerves? More importantly, what will you say to yourself in the future to make sure you interpret them as something positive that will help your performance?

Download all Performance Plans in the Champion's Playbook at:
OutperformTheNorm.com/books

WHY THEY WON

On one of the most storied franchises in sports, the New York Yankees' Derek Jeter ranks among one of the best. He's the club's all time leader in hits, doubles, games played, stolen bases, times on base and plate appearances. He's also a five-time World Series champion and a 14-time All-Star.[15]

You don't get to that level without playing through pressure-packed moments and being able to harness your nervous energy.

Much of this chapter centered on our interpretation of nerves. When Jeter was asked about his butterflies, here's how he responded:

"But that's good, though. When you have butterflies, it means you care. I think I'd wonder about myself if I didn't. If I stopped having butterflies, then I wouldn't play anymore."

He saw his nervous energy as a positive that would help his performance and it made a massive difference in his play on the field. He added:

"I haven't been around here this long by thinking negatively, you know what I mean?"

10

PLAYING TO WIN
VS
PLAYING NOT TO LOSE

An Outperformer is so consumed with what they want that there is no thought of what they're trying to avoid.

Do you know of any athletes who have gotten labeled as a "choker?" Usually, this happens when they're playing not to lose instead of playing to win. It's a simple mindset that separates those who shine from those who shrink under pressure.

If you're a football player, you sometimes see this with the "prevent defense." It's a strategy that teams use late in the game after they've built up a big lead. I understand the logic of *why* they do it but I often joke that the only thing the prevent defense does is *"prevents you from WINNING."* The reason is because the team *built* their lead playing a certain way. Why go away from that? Why shift from playing aggressively to playing passively?

There was no better example than the 2017 Super Bowl between the Atlanta Falcons and the New England Patriots. The Falcons built a 28-3 lead early in the second half but then took their foot off the gas. They started trying not to make mistakes (playing not to lose) instead of trying to make touchdowns, field goals and stops on defense (playing to win). *They stopped doing what made them successful.* Sure enough, the Patriots engineered the greatest comeback in Super Bowl history.

To grasp this concept you have to understand how our brain actually works. You can't not think about something (yes, I realize that's a double negative). But if someone has given you the advice of not to focus, or not to think about something, they don't understand how our brains are wired. Even if you're telling your brain NOT to focus on *"something,"* all that registers with the brain is *"something."*[16]

For example, you've qualified to play in a national-level tournament and there will be bigger crowds than you've ever seen. Telling yourself, *"don't focus on the huge crowd,"* or *"don't think about all the people in the stands"* will register in your brain ONLY as *"huge crowd"* and *"all the people in the stands."* It will be counterproductive to what you're trying to do. Although it's something you're trying to avoid, your brain will be consciously focused on the wrong thing.

You have to take that focus and redirect it to something else. That's what playing to win vs. playing not to lose is: striving for a positive outcome instead of fearing a negative result. It's a simple, yet powerful, distinction. Every Outperforming athlete you've ever seen perform well under pressure has a mentality of playing to win. I guarantee it.

You know from the Introduction that I played football, basketball and golf in high school. Here's how playing to win vs. playing not to lose might have looked for me:

Wide Receiver on the football team:

"I will run a strong route and catch this pass"

vs.

"I hope I don't lose my footing on the wet field and drop the pass."

(Brain hears: *"strong route, catch the pass"* vs. *"lose my footing, drop the pass"*)

Shooting Guard on the basketball team:

"I want the ball in my hands at the end of the game"

vs.

"I'm not going to think about missing my free throws."

(Brain hears: *"I want the ball"* vs. *"missing my free throws"*)

Golf:

"I'm going to stripe this drive down the middle of the fairway"

vs.

"I don't want to hook it in the water left."

(Brain hears: *"stripe this drive, middle of the fairway"* vs. *"hook it, water left"*)

As you see, you can apply this to ANY sport. When you're re-directing your focus, you want to think in terms of the positive actions that will give you the best possible chance of achieving your outcome. This will always be better than trying to avoid a negative result.

Lastly, like all skills in this book, playing to win needs to be in-grained every single day in training and in practice. The reason people get labeled as "chokers" is because mistakes are magnified under intense pressure, as is mental weakness. If you cannot keep a playing to win mindset when the stakes are low, there's no chance you'll be able to do it when the stakes are high. But you'll find that consciously, continuously redirecting your focus to the positives will eventually make it second nature and automatic, even in the biggest games and competitions.

GAME RAISING REMINDERS

✓ Playing to win vs. playing not to lose is striving for a positive outcome vs. fearing a negative result.

✓ Your brain can't not think about something. Focus needs to be redirected to what you WANT to happen.

✓ Mistakes are magnified under pressure. Make playing to win a regular goal of yours in practice and training. You'll see the results when it matters most.

PERFORMANCE PLAN

❶ List 3 examples of playing to win vs. playing not to lose in your specific sport (and specific position, if it applies). Try to think of real-world scenarios you will encounter and what you will say to yourself during these times to ensure you're PLAYING TO WIN.

Download all Performance Plans in the Champion's Playbook at:
OutperformTheNorm.com/books

WHY THEY WON

At the 2016 Rio Olympics, gymnast Laurie Hernandez showed hundreds-of-millions-of-people what it meant to PLAY TO WIN. She whispered three words out loud to herself *seconds before* her balance beam routine, one of the most important competitions of her life:

"I got this."

Indeed, she got it, nailing the routine and helping lead the U.S. to a first place win.

Everyone saw this powerful example of positive self-talk and the Twitterverse blew up with people saying how they were going to use *"I got this"* in their own lives to generate more courage and confidence under pressure. It has even led to a book deal for Hernandez, titled *"I got this,"* all based on her playing to win mindset that fueled an epic performance when it mattered most.[17]

11

OVERCOMING OVERTRAINING AND BURNOUT

An Outperformer is fully charged when everyone else is drained.

I'm sorry to be the bearer of bad news but if you play sports for any amount of time, you're going to go through periods where you feel burned out and overtrained. It's inevitable and is a natural byproduct of high-performance athletics.

But keep this in mind – the elite and professional athletes you see on TV have an offseason and they USE IT. They know they need to recharge their physical and mental batteries if they want to perform their best because they cannot continue to put themselves through the daily, weekly, monthly and yearly rigors of training and competition without getting burned out and overtrained, mentally AND physically.

Why should you be any different?

You may be in a position where your training is, more or less, "year-round." Without offering my opinion on whether I agree with this approach, your best way to combat overtraining and

burnout is to use the "R-R-R Strategy." I have seen it work won-
ders for numerous high-level clients of mine.

The first R stands for *Recharge*. Think of your mental and physical batteries like your cell phone. When you talk, text, play games
and use social media, the battery on your cell phone gets drained,
right? Then, at night, you plug it in and it recharges to full
strength. The next day, the same thing happens. For the most part,
you can keep this balance of energy depletion of repletion, but
true burnout and overtraining happens when you've continually
drained your batteries to the point that your cell phone is "dead"
and completely out of power. It has nothing left to give because
you haven't scheduled the time to recharge it.

Your mind and body are the same way. Especially *during* the
season, regularly recharging your physical and mental batteries to
full strength is something you have to do.

Now, I get it: You're reading this book because you're a go-
getting, Type-A, competitive athlete with a burning desire to improve. Not a lot of athletes want to hear this, especially if they're
in the grind of the season, but *more* is not always *better*. Sometimes
it's best to step back and take some rest and relaxation. Go do
something that allows you to totally disengage, mentally and
physically, from your sport. There is no set period of time for this
– it could be an hour or it could be an entire day (if you are *really*
feeling burned out).

Doing this requires you to resist the temptation to think:

"If I take a day off, it's going to set me back so much!"

Yes, I've seen this waaaay too many times (and experienced it
myself). You need to CALM that voice in your head and think

about the upside. How much better are you going to perform when you're recharged and operating at full strength?

Answer: A lot.

The second R is to *Remove* the pressure. There's obviously a physical pressure in athletics but often it is the mental pressure that leads to burnout. This pressure can either be self-imposed or from others. I've talked plenty in this book about detaching yourself from outcomes. The pressure to deliver outcomes is what's contributing to your burnout. The remedy to this is usually to remember WHY you got involved in your sport to begin with – was it really because you were concerned with wins, losses, titles and outcomes, or was it because you had fun with the sport and enjoyed playing it? Remind yourself that, even with the brightest lights on the biggest stage, it IS possible to strive for the outcomes you want AND have fun in the process!

The third R is to *Reassess* your goals. After you take a step back to recharge your batteries and remove the pressure, it is a good idea to reassess what you genuinely want to achieve and accomplish. Are your goals still YOUR goals? Has anything changed? Where are you now and where would you like to go?

This is best done when your mind is fresh. When I'm in the thick of training for an Ironman triathlon and I'm mentally strained and physically sore, if you ask me how important my goal is to qualify for the world championships, I'll likely downplay it and tell you that it's not that big of a deal. I'm too engrossed in the fog of fatigue to give an honest, genuine answer. But if you give me the opportunity to recharge my batteries and remove the pressure of delivering that outcome, I'll tell you that it's *extremely* important. It's what gets me up in the morning and what motivates me to train.

You may have experienced something similar in the grind of your season. Many of us start out with lofty expectations at the beginning of the year but there is nothing wrong with stepping back, reassessing your goals and making sure the goals you set for yourself as still as important as they once were. You may scale your goals down, decide you've set the bar too low and ratchet them up, or keep them exactly the same, but reassessing your goals will give you greater clarity of what you truly want and how you want to Outperform.

GAME RAISING REMINDERS

✓ Even the highest performing athletes on the planet feel burned out and overtrained from time to time. It's normal.

✓ *Recharge* your mental and physical batteries. Don't fear taking short breaks every now and then. You'll perform better with your cell phone at full strength.

✓ *Remove* the pressure from outcomes. Remind yourself of why you started playing your sport to begin with.

✓ *Reassess* your goals. Use a fresh mind and perspective to determine where you are now and where you would still like to go.

PERFORMANCE PLAN

❶ What do you do to recharge your physical and mental batteries? What do you find intrinsically enjoyable that is outside of your sport?

❷ Why did you *start* playing your sport? Why do you *keep* playing your sport? Are these answers the same?

Download all Performance Plans in the Champion's Playbook at:
OutperformTheNorm.com/books

WHY THEY WON

If you haven't read Andre Agassi's autobiography, *Open*, I'd highly recommend it. In the book, even though he was famous, a multiple grand slam winner and one of the best tennis players in the world, he repeatedly says, *"I hate tennis."*[18]

And he means it. He really did hate tennis.

From the time he was old enough to swing a racket, tennis was his life. His father enrolled him in an intensive tennis camp early on and it became his identity. Yes, this approach did lead to tremendous success on the court, but as the pressure mounted, it fueled off-court drug use and rebellion.

It's not that intensive training and dedication is BAD (see the Michael Phelps example in *Practicing with a Purpose*), in fact, it's *necessary*. But Andre was so fearful that taking even *short* breaks would destroy his career that he was never performing with his physical and mental batteries at full strength. He also felt the pressure attached with the outcomes of winning matches and tournaments. It wasn't until the tail end of his career (when he started dating tennis legend, Steffi Graf) that he finally reassessed his goals, gained the proper perspective on tennis and started performing his best, on AND off the court.

12

STEPPING UP AND LEADING

*An Outperformer earns the trust and respect of others
by setting their own personal standard of excellence.*

Think of the most successful teams you've ever seen. Whether we're talking about baseball, basketball, football, hockey, lacrosse or anything else, you can almost always pinpoint one or two people that are driving the bus and are leaders of the team. They stand out and they step up. I'm hoping that if you haven't stepped up already, you will become one of those leaders. Here's how to do it:

The first step in leadership is to lead by example. I was born and raised in Minnesota and I'm a huge Vikings football fan. Not long ago we had a playoff game against the Seattle Seahawks and they brought out Bud Grant, a former Vikings coach, to do the pre-game ceremonial coin toss. We were playing the game outdoors at TCF bank stadium (our new indoor stadium was being built) and it was brutally cold. Temperatures were around zero degrees with wind chills of -15 degrees. Everyone thought we were going to get killed by the Seahawks and there were questions about whether we could handle the cold.

Bud Grant, even thought he's in his mid 80's in age, wanted to prove a point. The last thing he did before walking out to midfield for the coin toss was to turn to Roger Goodell (the commissioner of the NFL) and say:

"Hold onto my jacket. I want to show EVERYONE that the cold won't bother the Vikings!"

He performed the entire coin toss in a short-sleeved polo shirt when it was –15 degrees. The whole stadium erupted in applause and he became an instant social media sensation. And even though he hasn't been our coach for 30+ years, he was willing to put everybody else on his back and lead by example. It almost worked – the Vikings played a great game and should have won. All because one person was willing to step up and lead.

There are two different types of leaders: Appointed Leaders and Emergent Leaders. Appointed leaders are coaches, captains, teachers and principals. If you're an appointed leader, it's because somebody's given you that title. But there are also emergent leaders. These are not necessarily people that have titles (although they can be); they're people that everybody turns to in crucial situations when they need guidance and direction. These emergent leaders on teams are often the most important people in making the team successful.

The second principle of leadership is that leaders elevate the play of others. I grew up in the prime of Michael Jordan, who is almost universally considered the greatest basketball player ever. If you're reading this, you're likely too young to remember Jordan's career. Early on, he was winning scoring championships and dunk contests. He was a human highlight reel. But Jordan was widely criticized because he didn't get the best out of others. They thought he would never win an NBA championship because he was constantly putting people down and teammates thought he was too demanding and self-centered. It wasn't until he learned how to help others raise their game that he won his six NBA championships and truly became the G.O.A.T.

To elevate the play of others, you have to balance challenging and supporting people. This involves reading the personality of your teammates and what they respond best to. It's not a "one size fits all" approach. Some athletes may respond better when you challenge them to step up if they're not playing well. Others may need more support because if you challenge them openly, they could get defensive and actually play worse (play *not to lose*). It's all based on the makeup of the individual athlete. Great emergent leaders are able to observe others and "push the right buttons" to get the most out of them.

One of the biggest mistakes people make when they try to be a "leader" is to be too serious and critical in an effort to "set the tone" for the team (I did this when I was a captain). The tone is set by ACTIONS, specifically showing up every day and working hard without complaint. The tone is also set by the blend of support and constructive criticism given by the emergent leader. Strive for at least a 3-to-1 ratio of positive-to-negative feedback.[19] This elevates a team's play by reinforcing the positive and what someone is doing WELL.

The next principle of Outperforming leadership is role awareness. Great teams are puzzles and all the individual pieces need to fit together for it to work. Each of the pieces is critical because if one is missing, the finished product is incomplete. Leaders let everyone know how important and valuable they are to the puzzle. This includes everyone from the star player on the team, all the way to the last player on the practice squad. They all have a ROLE on the team and it's a leader's job to make them AWARE of how critical their individual contribution is to the team's success.

The last part of leading is to provide vision and direction. Anybody can lead when the team is winning and playing well, but Outperforming leaders are able to do this even when the team is struggling. If the team is in a slump, you have to be the one that steps up to speak that vision and direction and say:

"We may be struggling now but this is where we're going. We'll get it turned around!"

Doing this is not easy, especially when team morale is low and everyone doubts their ability, but athletic seasons are roller coasters, not train rides. All great teams need a leader who can provide vision and direction *through the ups and downs* that rallies people towards a shared goal.

GAME RAISING REMINDERS

✓ Lead by example. Never ask someone to do something you're not willing to do yourself.

✓ Appointed leaders have a title. Emergent leaders have the trust and respect of others.

✓ Great leaders elevate the play of those around them by balancing the supporting and challenging of teammates. Strive for a 3-to-1 ratio of positive-to-negative feedback.

✓ EVERYONE on the team has a role and should be aware of how critical their individual contribution is to the team's success.

✓ Outperforming leaders provide vision and direction at all times, but especially when the team is not playing well.

PERFORMANCE PLAN

❶ Who is one of your favorite leaders? What specific characteristics do they display that makes you look up to them?

❷ What does it mean to you to lead by example? How will you demonstrate this to others around you?

❸ What type of feedback (positive or negative) do you like to receive on your performance? How can you use this to better lead others?

Download all Performance Plans in the Champion's Playbook at:
OutperformTheNorm.com/books

WHY THEY WON

Not many people think of Marcus Mariota, NFL quarterback of the Tennessee Titans, when they think of great leaders in sports. He's soft-spoken, humble (almost to a fault) and never draws attention to himself.

THAT is exactly why he is such a great leader.

The Titans are an up-and-coming franchise in the NFL and Mariota is a big reason why. Here are some of key components to his leadership style:

- He's non-judgmental (*do you judge others by their actions?*)

- He leads by example by going above and beyond (*are you the first one to arrive and last one to leave?*)

- He genuinely cares about people (*do you empathize with others?*)

- He knows what he wants and has a strong attention to detail (*do you have a crystal clear vision?*)

- He's real and authentic [20] (*are you 100% yourself, anywhere and everywhere?*)

These things may sound simple but they're the epitome of putting 'We' before 'Me.' Because of this, his teammates rally around him. They compete harder and his leadership makes them better. It translates to on-field results.

CONCLUSION

Congratulations on making it this far! You might not realize it, but if you're reading this right now, you're in the top 1% of all Outperformers.

It's true. Most athletes won't invest in mental training.

Some will invest but will never start.

A few will start but will get distracted, lose motivation and not finish.

Only the best of the best make it to this point and that's YOU. It's why only a fraction of a percentage of athletes unlock their true potential and compete at their individual highest level. Well done, Outperformer!

There are three final takeaways I'd like to give you:

1. Trust the Process.

This book should be referenced, not read. Fictional story-telling books are typically read once and discarded. When you reference something, it acts as an ongoing resource for your growth and development. That's how you should look at this book.

Caution yourself against expecting overnight results. Early on in the book, I compared mental training to physical training, where you can't expect to be strong from lifting weights one time. It's the repeated discipline that yields results.

Mental "conditioning" is exactly the same. Just like lifting weights, if you don't do it for a while, when you come back you realize that you're not as sharp and you've lost strength. But you regain it rapidly once you start up again, and if you stay consistent, you surpass your prior level of performance.

I can personally guarantee that if you commit to referencing this book, your mental "strength" will continue to grow in athletics, academics and life.

2. Remember WHY.

Assuming that you follow the first step, you're going to achieve higher and higher levels of success. With this comes a certain weight, and pressure, to Outperform. More people will be looking at what you're doing (and, thus, more critics) and the outcomes *seem* to have bigger consequences.

Your rise in success requires you to have an increased focus on WHY you started playing your sport in the first place. Any athletes you've ever seen compete in the NBA Finals, Super Bowl, Masters, Wimbledon, Stanley Cup, World Series or Olympics have utilized this strategy. How else do you think they can handle the scrutiny of performing in front of millions on people?

You might not be at that level – yet – but the same principle applies. If you can find the fun and joy in competing at the highest levels, your success, and fulfillment, will be unparalleled.

3. Never Underestimate Yourself.

Self-limiting beliefs are the governor on our individual potential. We are ALL capable of much more than we realize. In the *Unleashing the Alpha Dog* chapter, I compelled you to use vicarious experiences to enhance your confidence. Whatever you are looking to do in sports is within your reach. Someone has almost certainly done it before and it's unlikely this person is much different than you are.

The key to doing this is to start "stacking" your accomplishments (I'm sure you already have plenty!). Michael Jordan never set out to be the greatest basketball player of all time. He was cut from his high school team as a sophomore and his initial goal was simply to make the team. That was ALL he cared about. He turned the cut into motivation and said:

"Whenever I was working out and got tired and figured I ought to stop, I'd close my eyes and see that list in the locker room without my name on it."[21]

He made the team the next year. Then he became an all-state player. Then he received a scholarship to North Carolina. Then he won an NCAA championship. Then he was drafted into the NBA. Then he won an NBA title (and 5 more after that).

Making the team was a catalyst. It was the spark that lit a fire.

I'm not advocating that everyone reading this is going to play in the NBA. The fact is, only about .025% of high school basketball players ever play professionally.[22] But I want you to embrace the mindset of never underestimating what you are capable of accomplishing. Have HUGE aspirations! Wherever you are in your journey as an athlete, focus on taking the next step. It's the path to excellence that all Outperforming athletes before you have taken. If you continue to do that, there's no telling where you may go.

Wishing you all the best in athletics, academics and life,

Scott

SUMMARY GUIDE

COMMIT. COMPETE. SUCCEED.

1. Don't be interested. Be COMMITTED. It is an initial decision that must be made.

2. When you COMPETE, give all of your energy, focus, and effort. When you do this, you'll be able to handle any result.

3. To SUCCEED, there is no maintaining. Stay hungry and continue to challenge yourself with loftier goals and ambitions.

OWNING AND SMASHING YOUR GOALS

1. Outcome Goals are great because they provide motivation and direction, but you only have indirect control over them. Performance Goals are based on improving your own individual previous standards of performance, and they fuel Outcome Goals. Process Goals are ALWAYS 100% in your control, and they are the activities that will lead to achievement of your Performance Goals.

2. Make sure goals are yours. No one else's. Own them!

3. Any goal is realistic if you construct an intelligent plan to accomplish it.

MASTERING MOTIVATION

1. Posture affects physiology. Stand tall. Head up, chest out, shoulder blades back, and walk and talk like you're a real deal Outperformer.

2. Pick out your favorite motivational quote and have it visible DAILY. Your locker, backpack, phone wallpaper, car, bedroom, wallet, purse, etc., are all great examples.

3. Strategically and intentionally use your favorite media (movie scenes, songs, videos, podcasts, book passages, etc.) to pick you up when you're not on your game and feeling your best.

PRACTICING WITH A PURPOSE

1. Outperformers get more return (performance improvements) from their investment (time and energy). That's a big reason why they achieve world-class levels.

2. Chunk it out. Take ONE specific component of your technique that you're trying to improve and isolate it. Give it your 100% singular focus and effort. Then, rinse and repeat for the other components.

3. Slow it down to the point that you can execute any form or technique change absolutely perfectly.

UNLEASHING THE ALPHA DOG

1. Confidence is a good thing. It's necessary. It's arrogance under control.

2. Focus on your Power Posture. It'll immediately change your confidence at any point in time.

3. Make your preparation a dress rehearsal for game day and trust it! The more you mimic the specific demands you'll face, the better you'll be.

4. Use Vicarious Experiences. If someone else can do something, so can you!

5. Use imagery. Create the competition vividly in your mind, incorporating as many of the senses as possible. See it, feel it, hear it, smell it, experience it.

DEVELOPING GRIT

1. Be self-aware of your daily thoughts. Are they making you better or making you worse?

2. Avoid social comparison, and if you must do it, make sure it's motivating you.

3. Don't cut corners. The last 10-20% of doing something that you don't want to do flexes and strengthens your grit muscle.

4. Each day, lay ONE brick, perfectly. Eventually, you'll have a wall.

BUILDING BULLETPROOF RESILIENCY

1. If you ever feel like adversity is getting the best of you, use Countering. Be a lawyer and present a factual counter argument to the case going on in your own head.

2. Establish a reference point for a time when you've overcame great adversity in your life. Continually come back to it and say, "If I've done it before. I can do it again."

GETTING IN THE ZONE

1. Have a disciplined pre-competition routine and execute it the same every time.

2. Find a challenge in everything you do. If the competition is easy, create one.

3. Know your ZOF (Zone of Optimal Functioning) and use breathing and movements to raise or lower your arousal level.

4. Control the controllables! Worrying about anything other than you is irrelevant.

5. Avoid negative self-talk. Use a short 1-3 word phrase for positive reinforcement.

6. Be present. Be crystal clear and focused on what is happening RIGHT NOW.

HARNESSING YOUR NERVOUS ENERGY

1. Outperformers INTERPRET their nerves as a positive that will help their performance, whereas 'The Norm' sees nerves as a negative that will hurt their performance.

2. Identify your ZOF and be intentional about raising or lowering your arousal level to where you perform best using breathing, movements and music.

3. Remove the outcomes and focus on the actions that are 100% in your control.

PLAYING TO WIN VS PLAYING NOT TO LOSE

1. Playing to win vs. playing not to lose is striving for a positive outcome vs. fearing a negative result.
2. Your brain can't not think about something. Focus needs to be redirected to what you WANT to happen.
3. Mistakes are magnified under pressure. Make playing to win a regular goal of yours in practice and training.

OVERCOMING OVERTRAINING AND BURNOUT

1. Even the highest performing athletes on the planet feel burned out and overtrained from time to time. It's normal.
2. *Recharge* your mental and physical batteries. You'll perform better with your cell phone at full strength.
3. *Remove* the pressure from outcomes. Remind yourself of why you started playing your sport to begin with.
4. *Reassess* your goals. Use a fresh mind and perspective to determine where you are now and where you would still like to go.

STEPPING UP AND LEADING

1. Lead by example. Never ask someone to do something you're not willing to do yourself.

2. Appointed leaders are given a title. Emergent leaders have earned the trust and respect of others.

3. Great leaders elevate the play of those around them by balancing the supporting and challenging of teammates.

4. EVERYONE on the team has a role and should be aware of how critical their individual contribution is to the team's success.

5. Outperforming leaders provide vision and direction at all times, but especially when the team is not playing well.

FROM ATHLETICS TO ACADEMICS

Sports teaches you transferrable lessons about LIFE. Every one of these 12 chapters can easily be repurposed from competing on your athletic "field of play" to competing in the classroom.

I'm not going to preach at you about the importance of getting a good education and trying hard in school. You're an Outperformer and I assume you know these things already. What I WILL do is give you a few helpful tips to take these skills from sports to school.

FOCUS AND BE PRESENT

How well do you perform athletically when you're distracted and thinking about something else? Probably not well at all. But we all know what it's like to study or take a test and not be fully engaged with what we're doing. Then, we wonder why our results aren't what we want them to be.

Concentration and focus are learned skills and we must USE them if we're going to Outperform in the classroom. Make it a daily practice of challenging yourself to be as present as possible in school. The same way that you take it "one shot at a time" in athletics, strive to take it "one problem at a time" on homework and tests. Just like the ROI discussed in *Practicing with a Purpose*, you'll receive a greater performance return (learning and grades) from your investment (time and energy) when you have this singular focus.

USE A PEAK PERFORMANCE ROUTINE

In *Getting in the Zone* you learned the value of routines and how doing something the same way every time brings familiarity and success. Use the same strategy for studying.

Things to consider:
✓ Study in the same place
✓ Listen to the same music, or no music at all
✓ Drink or eat the same thing before or during (something healthy to fuel your body and nourish your brain!)
✓ MINIMIZE DISTRATIONS (silence your phone!)

I understand this can be an inexact science. Sometimes you may have to study late at night or early in the morning, or possibly in different locations, but having a consistent peak performance routine matters. When you do something the same way it signals to your brain that it's "GO TIME." It helps you to focus and lock in.

Lastly, and most importantly, please minimize distractions. Trust me, your life will go on if you're disconnected from your phone for an hour to study! Don't make it more difficult than it needs to be :-)

LEARN FROM THE BEST

In athletics, you must raise your game when you compete against bigger, faster, stronger, more-skilled players. Academics are the same way.

My brother is an intelligent, highly "talented" test-taker. He scored a 34 on his ACT test, a 1500 on his SAT test and was captain of the Knowledge Bowl team in high school. I'm the polar opposite; I was not born with that test-taking "gene." So, when I asked my brother if he would help me study to get ready for the GRE test (the general exam you must take to be accepted into graduate school), I knew we were playing in completely different leagues.

At first it was hard for me to not feel inferior to him as we went through sample questions for the test. *He just made everything look so EASY!* But as he explained to me his process for arriving at answers, the light bulb went on. It started to make more sense and I got better. I didn't ace my GRE but I got a score that was good enough to have my pick of graduate schools.

To me, this was like having a professional athlete personally coach me in my sport. What I learned from him was *invaluable*. My advice is to always surround yourself with others that will make you better. Whether this is a tutor, a study group or staying after class to get help from a teacher, it will raise your game and bring out the best in YOU.

FIGURE IT OUT

One of the additional insights from Gladwell's book, *Outliers*, was that students who were willing to work on math problems for longer significantly Outperformed students who gave up easily and asked for help.

Now, this may seem counter-intuitive to my previous point about learning from the best. It's not. There are advantages to surrounding yourself with others who will pull you up, but just like

Developing GRIT, it's also important to work hard and persevere until you *figure it out.*

This is becoming less natural in our google-ized society. If you want an answer, you search for it or ask Siri. You'll know within seconds. But true mastery comes on the other side of struggle and there is a distinct difference between when an answer is *given* versus when it's *earned.*

The next time you're doing homework, ask yourself whether you've really stayed gritty to earn the answer or whether you gave up too early and asked someone to give you the answer. It's a fine line and only you will know.

OUTPERFORMING RESOURCES

12 Individual Performance Plans in the Champions Playbook

Peak Performance Assessment

A hidden secret the pros use to stay motivated (it's controversial and

not mentioned in the book)

Special "Why They Won" Webinar

MORE video + audio training!

For instant access please visit:

OutperformTheNorm.com/books

Yes, the bonuses are free. Go get them now.

ABOUT THE AUTHOR

SCOTT WELLE is a #1 international best selling author, speaker and founder of Outperform The Norm, a global movement that coaches athletes and business leaders to raise their game and perform at the highest level.

While the rest of the competition is playing not to lose, Scott teaches people to play to win. His proprietary "Commit / Attack / Conquer" formula ensures people fall asleep at night knowing they are making the most of their precious days on this planet. For this, Fox 9 in Minneapolis-St Paul has called him a *"Motivational Expert."*

Scott has always loved sports but felt he underperformed early in his career by not mastering the "mental game." After graduating with his Master's degree in Sport Psychology, he made it his life's mission to coach people to higher levels of performance and not let others repeat his mistakes. Throughout this process, he's realized how the same mental principles that allow athletes to be successful will allow business leaders to achieve exceptional results, and this formed the foundation for Outperform The Norm.

Now, Scott's eight best selling books, articles, videos and podcasts inspire hundreds of thousands of people worldwide and students in over 35 countries have taken his online courses. He is an adjunct professor at St. Olaf University and serves on advisory committees of three national level organizations. He regularly coaches top performing executives, sales professionals and entrepreneurs, as well as elite athletes, all with one common goal: to OUTPERFORM.

Scott enjoys pushing his own physical and mental limits, completing five Ironman triathlons, 29 marathons, R2R2R (47 miles back and forth through the Grand Canyon) and a 100-mile ultra marathon run. He is very close with his brother, Jason. Together they "plod" at least one marathon together each year, laughing the whole way.

Please visit him at ScottWelle.com

ACKNOWLEDGEMENTS

This is the ninth time in my life that I've sat down to write the acknowledgements section after completing a book. It's never easy. These pages are a culmination of my education and experiences in sport and life, and how do you possibly recognize everyone who has contributed value to *that* and taught you something?

You don't. But I'll still try.

To my earliest sport psychology mentors in graduate school, Dr. Barry Joyner, Dr. Dan Czech and Dr. Kevin Burke, thanks for the mentorship and for the push along the way.

To my family, your influence is beyond words. Mom, I miss you. I try to be the man that you raised every day. Dad, thanks for getting me started in sports and for telling me I was good enough to take the last shot. Jason (Beef), you know your role in my life. I wouldn't be here without you. JoAnna, thanks for making me *want* to be my best. Moby, our dog, thanks for sleeping on the chair next to me as I worked tirelessly through these final edits :-)

To my coaching clients with whom I've been privileged to work throughout the years (there are too many of you to name), I've probably learned as much from you as you have from me. Thanks for the lessons.

To my friends, Justin, Diane, Adam, Missy, Kim, thanks for the support. We've had a lot of good times and crazy adventures. You guys rock.

Lastly, I love sports and I will continue to watch, observe and study them until the day I die. So, thank you to all the athletes who train and compete at any, and every, level. The area of performance enhancement will always be a wet canvas that is continuously being painted but I appreciate learning from you, firsthand, about what it takes to Outperform.

REFERENCES

1. Larkin, W. K. (2016). *Every cell in your body "hears."* Retrieved from http://appliedneuroscienceblog.com/every-cell-body-hears

2. *Tom Brady.* Retrieved from https://en.wikipedia.org/wiki/Tom_Brady

3. Neason, M. (2013). *Outcome goals vs process goals.* Retrieved from http://www.sportpsychologytoday.com/sports-psychology-articles/outcome-goals-vs-process-goals/

4. Borden, S. (2016). *The remarkable rise of Leicester City.* Retrieved from https://www.nytimes.com/2016/05/01/sports/soccer/how-leicester-city-went-right-side-up.html

5. Cuddy, A. (2012). *Your body language shapes who you are.* Retrieved from TED Global, 2012.

6. Gladwell, M. (2008). *Outliers: The story of success.* Little, Brown and Company.

7. Coyle, D. (2009). *The Talent Code: Greatness isn't born. It's grown. Here's how.* Random House Publishing.

8. Haney, H. (2012). *The big miss: My years coaching Tiger Woods.* Crown Archetype.

9. Gallo, C. (2016). *3 Habits of peak performers, according to Michael Phelps' coach.* Forbes.

10. Mautz, S. (2016). *9 success lessons from Usain Bolt's absurd Rio performance.* Retrieved from https://www.inc.com/scott-mautz/9-success-lessons-from-usain-bolts-absurd-rio-olympics.html

11. He, E. (2017). *After the hit: How Jack Jablonski is living life to the fullest despite paralysis.* Retrieved from http://dailytrojan.com/2017/04/11/hit-jack-jablonski-living-life-fullest-despite-paralysis/

12. Price, S.L. (2017). *The complex rise of Sloane Stephens.* Retrieved from https://www.si.com/tennis/2017/09/12/sloane-stephens-us-open-title-family-kamau-murray-injury-recovery

13. Whittle, M. (2016). *The pre-game routine that makes Steph Curry the best in the NBA.* Retrieved from https://www.theguardian.com/sport/2016/apr/18/steph-curry-golden-state-warriors-nba-pre-game

14. (2017) *The biological effects and consequences of anxiety.* Retrieved from http://www.anxietycare.org.uk/docs/biologicaleffects.asp

15. Lennon, D. (2012). *Derek Jeter is still motivated – everyday.* Retrieved from https://www.newsday.com/sports/columnists/david-lennon/derek-jeter-still-is-motivated-every-day-1.4054463

16. McGowan, K. (2004). *Mind control: Unwanted thoughts.* Retrieved from https://www.psychologytoday.com/articles/200401/mind-control-unwanted-thoughts

17. Hernandez, L. (2017). *I got this: To gold and beyond.* HarperCollins.

18. Agassi, A. (2010). *Open: An autobiography.* Vintage.

19. Positive Coaching Alliance. *Phil Jackson on the magic ratio.* Retrieved from http://devzone.positivecoach.org/resource/video/phil-jackson-magic-ratio

20. Clark, K. (2017). *The collected stories of Marcus Mariota.* Retrieved from https://www.theringer.com/nfl/2017/9/5/16254050/marcus-mariota-tennessee-titans-stories-best-leader

21. Poppel, S. (2015). *Michael Jordan didn't make varsity – at first.* Retrieved from http://www.newsweek.com/missing-cut-382954

22. Georgia Career Information Center. (2006) *Dreaming of becoming a college or professional athlete?* Retrieved from http://www.gcic.peachnet.edu/newsletter/dec06/dec%20outlook/athletes.html

ALSO BY SCOTT WELLE

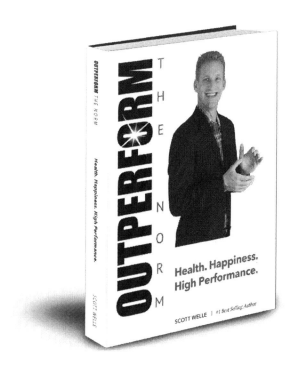

OUTPERFORM THE NORM

Health. Happiness. High Performance.

OutperformTheNorm.com/books

OUTPERFORM THE NORM
for Running

The 50 Best Tips EVER for Running
Fitter, Faster and Forever

OutperformTheNorm.com/books

OUTPERFORM THE NORM
for Triathlon

The 50 Best Tips EVER for Swimming,
Biking and Running

OutperformTheNorm.com/books

Made in the
USA
Columbia, SC